BRIGHT NOTES

THE OX-BOW INCIDENT BY WALTER CLARK

Intelligent Education

INFLUENCE PUBLISHERS

Nashville, Tennessee

BRIGHT NOTES: The Ox-Bow Incident
www.BrightNotes.com

ISBN: 978-1-645420-66-8 (Paperback)
ISBN: 978-1-645420-67-5 (eBook)

Published in accordance with the U.S. Copyright Office Orphan Works and Mass Digitization report of the register of copyrights, June 2015.

Originally published by Monarch Press.
James R Lindroth; Colette Lindroth, 1966
2019 Edition published by Influence Publishers.

Interior design by Lapiz Digital Services. Cover Design by Thinkpen Designs.

Printed in the United States of America.

Library of Congress Cataloging-in-Publication Data forthcoming.
Names: Intelligent Education
Title: BRIGHT NOTES: The Ox-Bow Incident
Subject: STU004000 STUDY AIDS / Book Notes

CONTENTS

INTRODUCTION TO WALTER CLARK

. . . .

A BIOGRAPHICAL SKETCH OF THE AUTHOR

Place Of Birth: It is surprising to learn that Walter Van Tilburg Clark, who has become famous as a writer of Western stories and as a man who can develop convincingly the character of a Western hero or villain, was in fact born in the East. He was born in East Orland, Maine, on August 3, 1909. His experiences in the West began early in his life, however, for he was only eight years old when his family moved from Maine to Reno, Nevada. His father became the President of the University of Nevada at that time, and held the position for many years.

His Early Schooling: The young Clark attended grammar school and high school in Reno, where his family continued to live. Eventually he entered the University there, and received both his B.A. and M.A. degrees. He forsook the West for some time after this, going back to the east coast where he attended the University of Vermont for two more years of graduate study. Here he pursued two interests, philosophy and English literature.

Teaching: After these experiences as a student, Clark decided to remain in the academic world in a somewhat different capacity; he taught school for ten years in Cazenovia, New York.

Here he showed the same versatility-of interests which later became evident in his writing; he served as basketball coach, advisor to the school dramatics group, and instructor. In 1933 he married Barbara Morse, a resident of Troy, Pennsylvania.

New Mexico: After looking at this much of Clark's life, it seems impossible that he could ever have become famous as a writer of Western stories. His early love of the West eventually reasserted itself, however, and after several years in Cazenovia he and his family moved to Taos, New Mexico. The Clarks lived in Taos only briefly, but it was long enough to convince Clark of something he had long suspected: he was, by nature if not by birth, intended to be a Westerner.

Nevada: Following his fairly brief residence at Taos, Clark moved on to Washoe Valley, in Nevada. Here he bought an old ranch, took up writing more and more seriously, and lived until 1951. He stopped teaching while in Nevada, and devoted himself full time to his writing, producing poetry, short stories, novellas, novels, and occasional nonfiction articles for national magazines.

San Francisco: Eventually Clark took up his academic career again, this time at San Francisco State College, where he is now a professor of English. He, his wife and family presently reside in San Francisco.

Publications: Early in his career Clark was principally a writer of poetry. He soon broadened his attempts to include short stories, and printed stories in national magazines throughout the 1940s and 1950s. He worked on his first novel, *The Ox-Bow Incident*, during 1937 and 1938; it was published in 1940, and immediately established its author as one of the more significant novelists of the decade. This was followed by *The City of Trembling Leaves*, which appeared in 1945, and *The Track of the Cat*, which was published in 1949. In 1950 he published *The Watchful Gods and Other Stories*, a collection of short stories which has received considerable critical attention.

INTRODUCTION TO WALTER CLARK

CLARK AND THE REALISTIC MOVEMENT

What Is **Realism**? To discuss the literary movement known as realism, one must first have a clear idea of precisely what **realism** is. In its broadest sense it can mean simply the accurate use of concrete details for the purpose of raising interest or creating an effect. So understood, **realism** has appeared in all periods of writing - Shakespeare's clowns are realistic, eighteenth-century English novelists such as Fielding or Defoe are quite realistic; even poets like Wordsworth or Robert Burns are realists if the term is used in its broadest sense.

Another Possibility: There is a second, more restricted kind of realism which one finds in writing where the characters are closely linked to, and affected by, their environments and by the events of their lives. This view of life usually rests on the idea that man knows only through his senses, only through what he can see or hear or touch or smell. Necessarily, the outside world must be of great importance in this kind of writing, since it is usually a major shaping force in the lives of characters; usually the reader gains a vivid sense of that outside world, and of the effect which environment and circumstances have on lives.

The Realistic Movement: There is a still more literal sense which the term "**realism**" may have, however. This applies specifically to a group of writers, beginning in the latter half of the nineteenth century, who have attempted common goals in the writing of fiction. The realists are noted for an attempt at objectivity, for letting their material tell its own story, rather than being somehow shaped or manipulated by the writer. They stress the ordinary life, the day-to-day existence of people who are not extraordinarily talented, or beautiful, or clever, or wealthy, or good - they write of the plain life of plain people.

The realists also tend to write about the immediate area in which they live, rather than putting their characters in some distant or exotic land; they stress the observation of objective reality rather than the creation of imaginative events or details. Above all, the realists stress the use of everyday language for their everyday people and lives; they eschew rhetoric in their attempt to let their people and their events speak for themselves.

Intent: The writers of the realistic movement, then, have simply refined and narrowed the general meaning of the word **realism** until they achieved characteristic styles and attitudes which set their writing apart from that which is only incidentally close to objective reality. They attempt to capture the essence of life as it is lived by the common man, and generally their literature is intended for, not the educated upper classes, but the common man himself.

Representatives: Emile Zola, the French nineteenth-century writer who wrote Nana, Germinal, and many other novels, is generally considered to be the father of the realistic school, along with his fellow-countryman Gustave Flaubert. **Realism** flourished in France with the activities of other writers, including Guy de Maupassant; in Russia it was developed by Tolstoy and

Turgenev. America has had writers who concentrate on realistic detail as early as Mark Twain (mid-nineteenth century); it is the turn-of-the-century novelist, however, who is chiefly remembered for the development of realism as practiced by Zola and Flaubert. The novelist-critic Henry James is famous for his attempts to capture "a slice of life"; his friend and colleague, William Dean Howells, is remembered for the "moral **realism**" which attempted to pursue everyday life while showing the moral significance of certain actions. Others, like the Englishman Somerset Maugham, preferred simply to chronicle life and leave the moral significance, if any, strictly up to the reader.

Recent Realistic Writers: The realistic novel has been popular in the United States ever since its first appearance. Some notable writers in the realistic tradition include James T. Farrell (*Studs Lonigan*), John Steinbeck (*The Grapes of Wrath, Tortilla Flats*), James Jones (*From Here to Eternity*), Norman Mailer (*The Naked and the Dead*), and many more.

Criticisms: The realistic novel has had a good deal of criticism during its existence. It has been attacked because it makes no attempt to uplift or inspire its audience; because it tells of the ordinary man rather than the extraordinary, complex, interesting one; because it oversimplifies life with its concentration on environment and psychology; and because it concentrates too much on ordinary **diction** and historical plot, rather than on inventiveness. In the second-rate realistic novel, any or all of these charges would probably have been justified. In the hands of a-Twain, a James, a Steinbeck - or a Clark - however, **realism** can do everything its detractors say it cannot. And, whatever its virtues or its drawbacks might be, it is still considered by most critics to be the predominant tendency in modern writing.

Clark As Realist: What kind of realist is Clark? Does he belong to the school of **realism**, or does he simply use accurate detail which is interesting, but not essential to his writing? A close look at his novels must put him in the realistic school in the tradition of Howells, Henry James, James Jones, Steinbeck. To be sure, Clark uses realistic detail extensively and skillfully. He is not merely painting an interesting picture with local color, however; he is writing a vivid, sometimes brutal, overwhelmingly moral story of men who are shaped by their environment and by what they themselves are. Thus he conforms to the more limited definition of **realism**, and can be put in the ranks of the realistic movement.

Freedom: Clark's characters are not really free. They are primarily shaped by the kind of lives they lead: they are violent men, attuned to struggle, and they are accustomed to acting fast and sometimes brutally to obtain their ends. They are shaped by their position in life, and they are also shaped by weaknesses within themselves; they lack courage, they lack the ability to think clearly, they lack the strength to oppose mass decisions. They are largely determined in their behavior by environmental and psychological factors.

Style: Clark's style corresponds to the characteristics of the realistic novel. His **diction** is simple, even slangy; obviously the characters are uneducated working men, and their conversation is appropriate to them. Since the entire book is told by Art Croft, the narrator, the language never becomes mannered or artificial. This is not to say that Clark is a tape-recorder, or that his language is dull or unpleasant; on the contrary, one can see that he has, with considerable artistry, shaped everyday language into an artistic instrument.

Objectivity: The use of a character within the book as narrator also allows Clark objectivity. His characters can function almost completely independently of their creator; the author is able to remove himself and let the material carry the story along.

Plot: As with style, plot in *The Ox-Bow Incident* is simple in the extreme. There is nothing fanciful, nothing of the imagination; Clark has simply taken an incident repeated on many pages of American history, and written a novel around it. Again, however, this must not be confused with reporting. If Clark's plot is historical, and if he simply follows literal time, he has done it for a purpose. In *The Ox-Bow Incident* he has taken ordinary men in a fairly ordinary situation, and has showed universal truths about humanity. One might very well disagree with Clark's conclusions, but one would not criticize the artistry with which he conveys them. Clark is a novelist of the realistic school, not a reporter.

INTRODUCTION TO WALTER CLARK

A Difficult Assessment: Since Clark is still a living, and indeed still a young writer, it is difficult if not impossible to accurately assess the full scope of his writing. He began writing poetry when still very young; he has written short stories, novellas, and three novels; he has contributed nonfiction articles to leading magazines, and two of his works were made into significant and influential movies. Obviously, then, Clark does not belong in any one category of American literature, but he has been recognized since the early 1940s as a serious creative writer and will continue to be so for some time to come.

The Status Of *The Ox-Bow Incident*: *The Ox-Bow Incident*, Clark's first novel, has received almost universal acclaim from the critics since it came out. Published in 1940, it reflected, as a good deal of the fiction of that era did, a mixture of moral and social concerns. The fact that it was put into an obviously Western setting, and dealt with the past, did not obscure its obvious relevance to the growing menace of Nazism. This setting, in fact, devoid as it is of any distracting details, revealed rather than obscured the morality-play quality of the story. There is evidence from Clark's letters that the work was received too completely, in his eyes, as a comment on Nazism; he has indicated more than once that he was concerned with the fact that this sort of injustice had occurred, and occurred often, in America. But whether or not its readers got the total message which Clark was trying to convey, they did get a good part of it, and *The Ox-Bow Incident* immediately found its place on the shelves of schools and libraries.

The Film: The dramatic structure and conflict-ridden plot were also seen as the ideal ingredients for another medium, and *Ox-Bow* was made into a movie soon after the novel was published. As a film, too, the stark story was well received; like "High Noon," this movie has come to be considered one of the all-time classic American movies. It can still be seen, of course, on the late movies on television; more significantly, however, it is still being mentioned, for purposes of comparison, in the movie columns of such influential critics as Judith Crist. Obviously, then, the story has revealed itself as being concerned with universal problems and universal moral concerns. It is no more an allegory of Nazism than it is a pulp Western. It contains the elements of the Nazi story and the Western, but it is much more; it is the story of men confronted by choice, and unable to make the proper decisions. Its survival, twenty-five years after its publication, indicates that it has continued speaking to all modern men rather than to just a few.

The City Of Trembling Leaves: Clark's second novel, published in 1945, was more limited in scope and was not so happily received either by the critics or by the public. The subject is quite different from *The Ox-Bow Incident*; it deals with the trials of the creative man, in this case a composer, trying to develop as a mature individual and to find his voice in his music.

The story line has been generally dismissed by the critics as being unsuccessful and too obviously autobiographical; what is of interest, however, is the view of nature which one sees in the novel.

The Role Of Nature: Clark has not moved his characters in space as he has in time; this is a modern novel, but again it is a story of the West, taking place in Reno, Nevada. Nature is here, as in Ox-Bow, really one of the most significant characters; Tim Hazard turns to the isolation of the mountains in order to discover his own identity. The mountains and the desert stand in direct contrast to the corrupted centers of man's greedy endeavors, in the form of Beverly Hills; they cleanse Hazard and purge him of his falseness and pretension.

Clark's Tradition: If the critics quarreled with Clark over his characterization of Tim Hazard, they did not quarrel with his view of nature. For Clark, when he sends Tim out to confront an overwhelming nature on her own terms, is in an American tradition which had its beginnings in Henry David Thoreau's *Walden*. Nature, in fact, serves the same purpose for both men; she is teacher and priest; she reveals the secret of true virtue, and man defines his own character only as he discovers the true character of the natural world in which he lives.

This view of nature is, of course, consistent with that seen in *The Ox-Bow Incident*. There one saw Croft turning to the isolation of a Western night when he was faced with a difficult decision; one saw him turning with relief from the sweaty, fume-laden confines of Canby's saloon to the clean, fresh outdoor air. The idea of nature, then, has been consistently developed from the first novel to the second, even if the skill of characterization or prose style has not.

The Track Of The Cat: This work, published in 1949, again saw Clark in the good graces of the critics. Once again he writes of the Western man of the soil; once again he is realistic in his approach, but here his symbolic view is even more apparent than it was in *The Ox-Bow Incident*.

Characters: The three major characters in this novel represent something of a distillation of the numerous characters in *Ox-Bow*. There is Arthur Bridges, who, like Davies, refuses to accept violence as a way of life and is mocked and eventually killed because of his convictions. His brother Curt is much like Tetley; he is materialistic, insensitive, crazy for the power to control people and events. Like Tetley, he eventually falls victim to his own nature; he dies when he overreaches himself and tries to command nature as he has commanded men. The younger brother, Harold; could perhaps best be compared to Croft. He is the most fully human of the three Bridges brothers; he best unifies the worlds of the ideal and the material. Like Croft, he is in part a spectator; he understands the motivations of the men he sees.

The Problem: The characters are similar, then, to those of *Ox-Bow*, and so is the moral preoccupation of the book. The problem which is presented is different, however; here Clark is concerned with the problems of a hostile natural world, represented by the mountain lion, and by the problems of the white man's mistreatment of the Indian, who is personified by the Indian worker Joe Sam. It is the mountain lion and Joe Sam who carry the major symbolic weight of the work. The lion has, in fact, been compared by more than one critic to the whale of Herman Melville's *Moby Dick*.

The Movie: Like *The Ox-Bow Incident*, *The Track of the Cat* was made into a movie. It, too, has had a long life in this medium; again, the story of man confronted by the evil of his own making has spoken effectively to a large audience.

The Watchful Gods And Other Stories: This collection, printed in 1950, contained a novella (the title story) and several previously printed shorter works. With *The Ox-Bow Incident* and *The Track of the Cat*, this collection is considered to be one of Clark's most significant accomplishments. A recent magazine article, considering influences on contemporary writers, includes *The Watchful Gods* as one of the more significant achievements of the '40s. The article stressed the influence which Clark has had on the young writers of the '50s and '60s; the author of the article, George P. Elliot, in fact indicates that Clark's influence through his short stories may be as great as that through his novels.

Themes: The themes of these stories are worth considering, since they are a continuation of those investigated in his novels. Clark again considers man's spiritual development, and the problem which each individual faces in his attempt to find his identity; he considers man's attempts to understand nature and to become a part of it; he also considers nature's refusal to accept man, and man's consequent isolation. In "The Indian Wall" one finds developed at length what had been a major consideration of *The Track of the Cat*. Here Clark pictures man as something passing, something unsteady, in direct contrast to the enduring qualities of nature. In "Hook," the reader discovers that this idea has been advanced one step further - man has disappeared from the story almost completely. Here Clark deals with a hawk as his major character; the story follows the hawk on his life cycle, from his birth to his death. The hawk is a magnificent bird, achieving the oneness with the rest of the world which the human characters in Clark's novels and stories never can achieve.

It is interesting to note that "Hook," which was printed in 1940, is very similar to another story, "The Rise and Passing of Bar," which he published three years later. In this story the main character is an animal rather than a bird, but again man has almost disappeared - that Clark should choose to write two stories so similar in so short a time indicates that this motif of the disappearance of man is a major interest of his.

Major Concerns: The rest of the stories in *The Watchful Gods* continue to develop these ideas. The major consideration, which can be found in Clark's novels and stories alike, is the idea that man must cease to be only a man if he is to achieve any success. Davies, in *The Ox-Bow Incident*, is the perfect example of the man who becomes an agonizing failure because he depends only on his human faculty, his reason. Croft, who is close to nature and who accepts the eternal significance of nature along with his own essential insignificance, is much more of a success. It is an unfortunate paradox for man that nature is reluctant to accept him on her territory, but nevertheless man must continue to strive for this oneness, even though he might never be successful.

Optimist Or Pessimist: *The Ox-Bow Incident* does not give a particularly happy picture of mankind, nor do most of Clark's stories. Man is thoughtless, greedy, driven by a desire for material gain and for power. But some men, at least, are reflective and sensitive; some have a capacity for learning from the world of nature which surrounds them. Therefore, though his view of life is essentially harsh, it cannot be said that Clark is a pessimist. He sees man's capacity for evil, but he also sees the other world, the world which can touch man and cleanse him of his faults. In this sense it is possible to place him in the tradition of American Transcendentalist writers like Ralph Waldo Emerson and Henry

David Thoreau (poets and essayists of the early 19th century) who saw men as being able to learn from nature. What Clark does not have, which Thoreau and Emerson did, is the conviction that beneath his wrong-headedness man is essentially good. Clark is not so convinced of this goodness; at times evil triumphs in his stories, at times it is a draw between good and evil, but never does good really remain triumphant over evil.

Realism: If Clark owes to the tradition of Emerson and Thoreau, however, he can also be seen as a descendant of the nineteenth-century realist Mark Twain. Twain and Clark have in common a love of nature; they also share a rather doubtful, sometimes cynical, view of man. Their fiction technique is also quite similar; both writers manage to evoke the spirit of the area they write about by filling their works with concrete, realistic details. Both men, too, are of the West; Twain became famous for his picture of the West and Middle West in such works as *Huckleberry Finn* and *Life on the Mississippi*. Clark, on his part, has captured the essence of a harsh, mountainous Western American landscape in *The Ox-Bow Incident* and *The Track of the Cat.*

Symbolism: But Clark is not only indebted to the 19th century; he is also very much a modern man. He uses symbol skillfully, especially in *The Track of the Cat* and *The Ox-Bow Incident*. In the latter, nature is nearly always symbolic of the mental condition of the men; the growing winter storm parallels the growing fury of the lynch mob, and the heavy snow which finally begins to fall must be considered as nature's disapproving comment on the activities which the men are about to indulge in. The "Ox-Bow" itself, that idyllic little valley in the mountains, can be seen as a symbol of the quiet beauty of nature, a direct contrast to the cruel carnality of the men who stop there.

Style: In style, one sees Clark as a completely modern writer. Like Ernest Hemingway, he writes simply and casually, concentrating on vivid detail and stripping his stories down to the minimum essentials. For this reason his works are both eminently readable and highly effective. The characters are memorable because Clark captures accurately the quality of colloquial speech, and the events are memorable because they are not obscured by extra details. He can indicate nuances of character with simple, characteristic gestures; an excellent example of this is the men in *The Ox-Bow Incident*, waiting uneasily for the posse to be formed, wandering around feeling their faces and occasionally spitting on the ground. After indicating a detail like this it is unnecessary for Clark to tell the reader that the men are nervous, or insecure, or afraid or uncertain; they have revealed their state to the reader by their actions.

Summary: Thus it can be seen that Clark's scope in writing is wide. He has proved his skill in several different kinds of fiction, and has inspired another medium, the movies. One can see in his works the influences of the major nineteenth-century American literary movements (Transcendentalism and **realism**), but one also sees a modern concern with symbol and compression of style.

THEME AND TECHNIQUE IN THE OX-BOW INCIDENT

Isolating The Element Of **Theme**: Although it is impossible to separate one element out of a work of fiction and discuss it completely in isolation, it is possible, for the sake of argument, to talk about one or another element of a work which the author has emphasized. There are, for example, works of fiction which we call adventure stories, or novels of manners, or novels of character; there are works that we remember primarily for their psychological study of character or for their **satire** of a manner of living or for their symbolic rendering of experience.

All elements of a fictional work must function together and must contribute to the meaning of the whole. Through analysis of these separate elements we can discover that meaning and the manner in which the work is made. However, in discovering how the work is made, we often discover that one or another of the parts is the dominant element and that the others function in support of it, contributing to the whole. The dominant element in *The Ox-Bow Incident* is the **theme** of violence and mob justice and the dilemmas which surround the basic conflict - of guilt and innocence, courage and cowardice, the identity of the good man and the bad.

What Is **Theme**? This statement of the theme of the novel is, of course, too narrow, too restrictive; it does not allow for all the elements of the novel, but limits the meaning of the work of fiction to a flat, aphoristic statement. Perhaps we can define **theme** so that we can understand how all the elements of the work of fiction participate in the meaning and how the concept of **theme** can be isolated. Theme is the meaning the story releases; it may be the meaning the story discovers. By **theme** we mean the necessary implications of the whole story, not a separable part of a story. **Theme** in fiction is what the author is able to make of the total experience rendered. And although there will be something general in the **theme** of a work of fiction, there will always be something unique there as well. We may, for the sake of convenience, be prepared to express the **theme** of a story in general terms, but we must always be aware of how the general statement has been modified, qualified, rendered unique by all the particular details of the story as it unfolds.

Theme And Technique: This definition of theme can be examined in terms of its implications for the technique of a novel, in order to clarify the relationship between **theme** and technique. We have said, for example, that the **theme** in a fictional work is what the author can make of the experience rendered. By answering the question of how the author makes an experience intelligible to the reader, we can see how the technical or formal elements of a story are used to convey the **theme** or content. Of course it is as artificial to make this distinction between form and content except for purposes of analysis as it is to separate out the single element, **theme**. We must be constantly aware of the wholeness of a work of literature while we analyze its parts.

In order to understand both that wholeness and to analyze the formal elements of *The Ox-Bow Incident*, it will be helpful to discuss its **theme** in relation to character and plot.

Theme And Character: Character is, in *The Ox-Bow Incident*, the chief means by which Clark conveys his **theme**, since, because of the nature of the experience of forming a posse, there is a tremendous amount of opportunity for portrayal of direct discussion of the dilemma. As a major element in fiction, character is obviously of major importance for **theme**. One matter to be kept in mind in reading is the kind of characters with which the story deals. If a writer like Henry Janes seems characteristically to portray highly sensitive, highly articulate men and women, we may feel justified in assuming that he finds a special value in the lives of such people. If a writer like Nelson Algren, on the other hand, populates his fictional world largely with pimps, streetwalkers, drug addicts, and sex deviates, this must indicate that Algren regards the lives of these outcasts as significant. F. Scott Fitzgerald's fascination with the very rich suggests a great deal about the meaning that experience has for him.

The mob which Clark presents to us is made of a number of individuals and also takes on its own character as a mob. It vacillates back and forth between various approaches to the problem of punishing Kincaid's "murderers," swayed by whichever voice is strongest, and gradually gaining sufficient momentum to be carried into the lynching almost without wanting to, and certainly without sufficient evidence or conviction that it is the right thing to do. It is carried by its need for an outlet in violence which must be satisfied.

The mob as a character in the novel is a faceless force made of individuals who lose their identity as individuals precisely because they are members of a mob. The few characters who do stand out from the mob are identifiable for the very reason that they do not go along with the mob as it is led to carry out the hanging. Davies, from the very beginning, stresses caution and justice; Croft is aware of all views on the subject and is able to comment on them; Tetley and Bartlett rouse the mob, Tetley eventually assuming leadership; Ma Grier in her demands for strong action is able to influence the mob; Gerald Tetley cannot stand his father's violent strength nor the actions of the "pack."

Each of the characters whom Clark delineates in detail, then, expresses a different view on the dilemma which the "posse" faces. In this way Clark is able to convey various views on the moral questions with which the novel deals. Various aspects of the thematic questions - views on justice and violence - are represented by the characters, and the characters become individualized by the very fact that they think differently from the mob. In this way, Clark is also able to comment implicitly (while commenting explicitly through Gerald Tetley) on the nature of the mob. The formal element, character, is Clark's major method of conveying his thematic material, and the thematic material determines the way in which Clark defines his characters, playing the individuals against the mob.

Theme And Plot: Plot is what the characters do and what happens to them. A first question about plot and **theme** is whether the author's characters do things, or whether things happen to them. The characters of Henry Fielding, on the one hand, do things, while things tend to happen to the characters of Thomas Hardy and Theodore Dreiser. This difference indicates something about the author's view of the extent to which man can control his destiny. We must also ask what kind of things the characters do and what kind of things happen to them. Hemingway's characters engage extensively in physical action, in the life of the senses, while the principal actions in the fiction of Henry James tend to be acts of intellect and conscience. Such tendencies suggest something about the author's sense of what kind of actions are most significant and most revealing.

Clark's characters are caught in a mob action which does not allow them to act as individuals and which swallows everyone except those who know how to feed it and use it for their own purposes. Davies and Osgood are not heeded, while Tetley, Bartlett, and Ma Grier are able to direct the mob's actions. As we have seen, the mob gains its own momentum, the need for violence demands to be satisfied, the few dissenters are silenced, and things happen almost without having been made to happen. Once set in motion, the action cannot be stopped, men must hang.

By the time the hanging occurs, it is almost an anticlimax. The tension between opposing forces fighting to win the mob has been so great, and the mob, once won by violence, is so resolute, that the arguments over the guilt of the three men and the hanging is anticlimactic. It is the natural result of the nature of the mob, not any longer a point at which a significant choice can be made: the possibility that they will let the men go exists, and creates a certain amount of suspense, but it is not strong enough to create a climactic situation. The **climax** occurred at some point earlier, when the posse was totally committed to fulfilling the threat of violence to revenge Kincaid's death.

The major concern of the novel is the dialogue between various characters about the nature of justice and the need for violent revenge, the satisfying of the men's need for violence, and the effect of the mob's action on some of the characters. Once set in motion, the mob moves on its own momentum to their satisfaction in the hanging. Although the reappearance of Kincaid is shocking to some, others are able to volunteer to join the sheriff's posse to find the "real" criminals. Davies is almost destroyed and Gerald Tetley and then his father, kills himself. The individual is affected by the mob, but the mob, after satisfying itself, no longer exists, and has never had a conscience.

Other Methods Of Discovering **Theme**: Just as the two major formal elements of *The Ox-Bow Incident*, character and plot, reveal the content of the novel - its meaning, the **theme** - so do all the other formal elements reveal the content. Style, tone, language, and point of view all function to convey the single meaning of the novel, and a careful reading will reveal the way in which **theme** is revealed through formal technique, and formal technique tailored to meet the needs of the thematic material.

THE OX-BOW INCIDENT

. . . .

PART ONE

EXPOSITION

The first of the five parts of *The Ox-Bow Incident* is a classic example of narrative **exposition** (the introduction of the themes, characters, situations, symbols and other material of which a narrative action is made). Casually, and in the manner with which we have become so familiar through the media of television and the movies, Clark moves us off the trail and into the saloon along with Art Croft and Gil Carter; we watch with Croft, who narrates the story, as the scene unfolds. And, as each new element of that scene strikes Croft's sensibilities and is relayed to us through him as narrator, we learn about the men, their surroundings, and their behaviour.

If we read carefully enough we can recognize in these first pages the matter of the entire novel - present but not yet expanded into its full narrative form. Everything is present here: nature, Croft's reactions to it, and its symbolic import in terms of men's actions; the character traits of some of the men involved in the main action of the novel - a basis for understanding their motivation and perhaps predicting their actions; the suggestion of guilt being imputed to the innocent; violence present in all of us - even in the relationship between two friends such as Croft and Gil Carter - making men capable of inflicting harm unless it is channeled into relatively harmless outlets such as a soon-forgotten brawl.

Comment: The Threat: The opening description of the weather can be read as symbolic of the events which are to happen in the novel. It is calm and lovely now, but there is a hint of instability in the air; the day is typical of the earliest spring - there is a threat of a possible return to winter. The narrator is aware of this and the reader notes the fact and stores it away for future reference. The storm which eventually breaks, in the men and the weather, is therefore not a complete surprise. Winter is not yet gone from the land nor are the pent-up emotions of winter thoroughly worked out of the men who have just finished spring round-up.

The Town Of Bridger's Wells: The town which the two riders approach is, like the rest of the setting, the kind of scene which could be found in any Western movie. As they approach they see a general store, the land and mining office, the saloon, a rickety hotel, two churches, and an assortment of houses. There is even the town drunk slouching along the street - Bridger's Wells, in other words, is exactly the kind of town which can be found in any of a hundred television or movie Westerns.

The Saloon: If the setting is typical of TV Westerns, so is the saloon which the men eventually enter.

This, of course, does not mean that Clark is careless or superficial in his writing; he has simply captured the essence of the American frontier town in the last century and is using a very simple and realistic setting as a background against which he can play out a much more complex story. It is not the Western setting which is of primary importance, but the drama of men struggling to understand and to live an ideal with which Clark is really concerned.

The Picture: The interior of Canby's saloon, where most of the early action takes place, is worthy of a closer look. Its decor is revealing of the mentality of its customers: the pictures on the wall reveal a capacity for sordidness and violence in this isolated little frontier town. The picture "Woman with Parrot" is particularly significant; it is not typical calendar art, with a seductive young girl enticing a clean-cut young man. Rather it is the portrait of an older, heavily sensual woman pretending to play with an "ugly" bird. It is an ugly picture of eternal frustration, for the man "sneaking up" on the woman will always be repulsed by her. What sensuality there is, then, is ugly and frustrated, just as the sensual lives of these men have been made ugly and frustrated by the frontier conditions.

The Poker Players: The four men playing poker are also indicative of the grim environment of the novel. They do not speak; they, like the ugly individuals in the picture, are without life or energy.

The Men: It is evident that the men whom we meet are not merely paste-ups of the stereotyped cowboy with whom we are all so familiar. The relationship between Croft and Gil reveals this immediately. They are good friends who live and work together and they understand the tension under which they have been cooped up together for months. They are very different personalities and as a result they have had their problems living together. They have even come to the point where they cannot put up with one another, but their friendship can bear the violence which is part of their nature as men.

Gil is revealed to us through his own words, reported by Croft, and through Croft's comments about him. But, as narrator, Croft cannot tell us about himself. We learn about him directly through what he says - his descriptions of what he sees, his comments about Gil, and his reactions to the action around him. We also learn about him through what Gil tells Canby about him.

Point Of View: Croft, the narrator, is not only a source of information about all of the characters and events of the novel, but about himself. This is a good place to begin to talk about the point of view of the novel. Since Croft is the narrator, his are the eyes through which we see everything and his consciousness is the one through which we receive all of our impressions. We must ask ourselves whether Clark has created a character whom we can believe and whose reactions we can trust, or whether we must judge everything we learn through Croft against what we know about his character. As I have said we learn about his character through everything he says, what he tells us he does, what he says he feels and through what Gil tells Canby. We must decide whether Croft is an objective narrator whom we can trust to give us a reliable view of things on the basis of which we can make a judgment as Clark asks us to, or whether we must re-interpret everything he tells us, filtering out his particular prejudices and character eccentricities.

We can begin to judge Croft's reliability by the honesty with which he reports Gil's feeling about himself (Croft) and his, to Gil, "peculiar" behaviour during the long hours they were cooped up on the range. Croft is a much more contemplative person than Gil; Clark will reveal more of Croft's sensitivity and contemplative nature as the novel progresses. These qualities, along with his honesty, in many situations, in admitting his inadequacies in dealing with the large moral issues presented, convince us that we can trust Croft to present a valid view of all sides of the dilemma of the novel.

The Scene And The Reality: In the first section of *The Ox-Bow Incident*, then, Clark sets the scene for all the ensuing events in the novel, and skillfully prepares the reader psychologically for everything which is to follow. The setting, as has been noted, is the traditional - in fact, the cliche - setting of the Western movie or story. From the very beginning, however, the reader of this novel realizes that it is not going to be another pulp Western, with the good guys on white horses and the bad guys on black; each character is complex, and no one is capable of being the single-handed savior of the town. The setting, too, is more complex than it might seem at first glance; the essence of the frontier community, with its advantages and disadvantages, is subtly indicated from the very opening passage.

Violence: The reader is made aware that everyone in this place has lived with violence, that violence has become a way of life for them. Gil looks on fighting rather innocently; he simply considers a fight a good way of expending excess energy. Croft, however, is aware of and repelled by some of this violence. He, unlike Gil, is aware of the excesses to which it can lead. All of the men in the bar are ready to fight, over anything or nothing; therefore, when the crisis of Kinkaid's death confronts them, their course is clear. Since the violence of fist fights is commonplace to them, the reader suspects that this new struggle will be a much more significant one-lynching seems the logical answer.

The Characters: But, if the book is no mere pulp Western, neither is it simply a study in violence. The men who live in this harsh and hostile environment are not simply animals. Each individual is complex, capable of reacting differently to different situations. This is what prevents the story from becoming stereotyped: the men live with struggle, they are confronted with murder, yet they have within themselves the capability to choose another path than mob justice. Croft, the narrator, through whose eyes the reader sees the setting and the action, is a good example of this complexity.

Croft's Character: The first thing the reader knows about Art Croft is that he is a cowhand. He lives up to the stereotyped ideas about cowboys; he is concerned with his horse, and aware of Blue Boy's reactions; he is anxious for the drinks, the poker and the companionship of Canby's saloon; he makes appropriately ribald remarks about the paintings there.

Croft's Sensitivity: Even from the beginning, however, the reader is aware that Croft thinks of more than what cowboys are "supposed" to think of - women and liquor and cards. He is, to begin with, highly sensitive to the beauties of the outdoor world he lives in. The detailed description of the opening scene of the novel indicates that Croft has an acute, observing eye, that he is aware of the light, of the wind, of the slightest change in the weather or the sky. He is also aware of the birds, and of the small animals which they see on their ride. From Croft's awareness of Gil's moods, the reader can also determine that the narrator is an accurate judge of character; he can tell that Croft will meet violence when he must, but that he would rather avoid it whenever possible.

His Shrewdness: From Croft's description of Moore, the foreman, the reader can tell that Croft is able to judge other men as well as his friend. Croft sees through him; he sees the fear underneath the apparent confidence. From the beginning of the novel, then, the reader is quite confident about Croft's ability to judge men accurately; he is also willing to accept Croft's judgment about men's actions, since he does not delude himself.

His Reflective Qualities: Two other essential points about Croft's character are revealed through Gil. We learn that Croft is, to some extent at least, a thinker; he is able to handle ideas, to think in abstractions when necessary and that he is a "loner," a man who trusts the outdoors more than he does the interior of rooms. He is also more honest than one might immediately expect.

Reliable Point Of View: From the outset, then, the reader sees in Croft a sensitive and intelligent man who is capable of judging his companions and their actions. He is not perfect himself, but he is honest; his is a reliable point of view from which to judge the other characters and the events of the book. He is not out of place in this frontier environment - his reactions are those of an outdoorsman and a man of the frontier - but he is more reflective than some of his companions.

Gil's Character: If Croft is described as a thin and fairly sensitive man, Gil seems to be just the opposite. He is big and strong and fond of getting drunk and fighting - at first glance he might seem to be the stereotyped thick-headed cowboy of the Late Late Show. Even Gil, however, is a complex character, as his reaction to the news of Rose Mapen indicates. He had obviously been in love with her, though he is reluctant to admit it; he, too, has sensitive feelings which he will not reveal to the outside world. Viewed from this perspective, his fighting becomes more understandable. He brawls to release his tensions, but he also brawls because he has been hurt by Rose, and has no other way of expressing himself. He, like Croft, is also essentially honest. If he is not as reflective as Croft, he is certainly not stupid; and he, like Croft, judges his own actions honestly.

Significance: Thus, from the very beginning of the novel, it is evident that *The Ox-Bow Incident* is not going to be just a typical Western. It is presented as a story about people, about their reactions to a set of incidents. The men are cowhands, but they are also individuals; they are capable of reacting in more than one way to any situation. The Western setting, rather than obscuring the significance of the action, reveals it; the setting is stripped to its essentials, and there is nothing to distract the reader from the overwhelming significance of the choices which the men do eventually make.

Mood: There is a distinctive mood, or attitude, coloring the first part of the novel. The characters are restless, filled with energy and looking for someplace to expend this energy. There is, in the description of the tawdry saloon and the down-at-the-heels town, a sordid air. There is also, however, a feeling of great peace. This is most obvious in the description of the trail, the mountains, in Croft's comments on the beauty of the air when he leaves the saloon. The mood at the beginning of the novel, then, is like the mood of the pre-spring weather in the story; it is changeable and undependable. There is a potential for beauty in the setting and for nobility in the men; there is also the potential for violence and ugliness in both. The reader wonders, as he does on a day in March, whether the storm will hit or whether calm will prevail.

Ox-Bow As A Western: We have mentioned the fact that various elements of the novel are standard ingredients of the typical Western, but in each case we have said that Clark does so much more than the usual with these elements. Clark wrote *The Ox-Bow Incident* with the problem of the stereotypes of the western in mind. He wanted to be able to use these materials, without being trapped by them, to write about something that concerned him. The novel was the product of a kind of "deliberate technical exercise" (letter dated Mill Valley, California, September 1, 1959).

THE OX-BOW INCIDENT

As we move from the end of Part One and the announcement of Kincaid's death, to the beginning of Part Two, the whole atmosphere of the novel changes. Part One was the beginning of a Western, subtly done, with the hints of other more important things to be considered. Part Two will actually begin the drama of a mob of men vacillating between choosing justice or violence, a **theme** more timeless and less tied to place than anything with which a Western usually deals. Clark has not written a Western but the story of a classic moral struggle which happens to be set in the American West.

Comment: Through the eyes of Croft, one sees Davies, the old man, as a man of reason, a man who insists on thought before action and who dislikes violence.

Farnley's Reaction: If Davies' words picture him as a rational man, Farnley's response heightens the unpleasant picture which the reader has of him. It

becomes evident that Farnley is not after justice at all, but simply wants an excuse to show off, to utter threats, and, perhaps, to kill someone.

Reverend Osgood: Another voice of calm is that of the Reverend Osgood. But Osgood is too "talky," too preachy, to make himself effective in this scene.

The Idea Of Courage. Croft, who as usual is observing all the action, makes some interesting comments here on the nature of courage. He realizes that Osgood is actually being quite courageous in the moral sense of the word, making himself speak up when he'd rather just remain quiet. He also realizes that Davies is perhaps the bravest man of the lot. And we learn through Croft's reflections that Farnley himself is only a coward making loud and violent, and quite unconvincing, protestations of his courage.

The Sheriff And The Judge: The suggestion that someone should call Sheriff Risley and Judge Tyler reveals the emotional climate in the town; the cowpunchers would not be sorry to see Risley, whom they respect, take over the situation, but they are indignant at the suggestion that Judge Tyler might tell them what to do. It is apparent to the reader that the cowhands, all men of action, men of the outdoors, men of comparative poverty, resent everything the Judge stands for. They resent his money, his social position, his identification with the life of the indoors, his stuffiness, and above all they resent his tendency to talk rather than to act.

Bartlett's Speech: Bartlett's speech is entirely emotional and inflammatory; as is usually the case with rabble-rousers, Bartlett exaggerates some details and invents some others in his eagerness to inspire the men to revenge.

The Response: In the course of Croft's analysis of Bartlett's speech, we learn two things about the mob: their shocked reactions to cattle stealing are largely artificial; and they probably have thoroughly guilty consciences of their own. These factors make them an easy prey to rabble-rousers like Bartlett and Farnley; to an extent, at least, many of them will decide on mob action simply in an attempt to cover up their own guilty pasts.

Significance: Gil's actions, and the new mention of lynching, are more significant than they might immediately appear. Gil's interest in the entire situation is really quite casual; he is not, as some of the others obviously are, a victim of much self-delusion. He is, however, not above suspicion himself - and he knows it. This is why he reacts so violently; he is, in fact, making an attempt at ingratiating himself with the crowd. Since he doesn't like Osgood anyway, the job is fairly easy for him.

The Attitude Toward Lynching: A new mention of lynching is important for two reasons. First, it is said almost casually this time, as though it was a widely accepted course of action. Second, it has been used as a threat; before, lynching had only been mentioned as a reprisal against the unknown murderers. This makes the violence much more local, and so more threatening; for months, everyone had been afraid that a local man might be the guilty party. Now the nagging fear that a local man might be the culprit has been made explicit, even though it is ostensibly done as a joke; in other words, neighbor has been set against neighbor.

Significance: The significance of Winder's appearance and his tirade in comparison to Bartlett's is quite clear. Through the two tirades, alike in tone but different in content, and through the fairly objective reflections of Croft, the author is making clear a point about the nature of men's reactions: when individuals are worked up about something they fall easy prey to anyone with a conviction, some rhetorical ability, and an emotionally fervent approach. The points which Bartlett brought up were at least partially linked to the situation; exaggerated and distorted as his discussion was, he at least talked about cattle rustling and murder. Winder's case, however, is something quite different; he is simply using the emotion-charged situation as an excuse to air his own private grievance and to elicit an emotional response toward his personal problems. The fact that the men listen to him at all is significant; it indicates that they have already begun to forget, in part, what the initial cause of their emotional upheaval was.

A Change In Tone: There is a second development, only partially related to the plot itself, which deserves mention at this point. From the beginning of the novel to the scene in Canby's saloon, there has been a gradual change in the weather, commented on occasionally by Croft. What had begun as a half-warm, half-wintry spring day has slowly developed into a calm before a storm. Even the sun has lost its warmth; the clouds are gathering over the mountains, and their dark undersides threaten snow. The significance of this development is clear; Clark intends the reader to make a comparison between the threatening weather and the ever-threatening mood and attitude of the men. There was still some possibility of calm, rational action at the end of Part One; now, after the inflammatory speeches by Bartlett and Winder and the self-centered reactions of Gil and Croft, this possibility has been greatly lessened. A storm is in the offing, both in the weather and in the men themselves. By this point in the novel it has become much more difficult to envision them reacting with either reason or any degree of compassion.

The Significance: While the two incidents in which Croft becomes involved on his way back from contacting Judge Tyler might appear at first glance to be merely comic relief, they are revealing of two things: the character of Croft and the characteristics of mankind in general. Croft, as usual, reacts with great sensitivity.

Little Tommy: Croft's behavior with the child is just as revealing of his pleasant and thoughtful character. He is concerned about the boy for he knows the boy is little more than a baby, far too young for the kind of activity he's watching. He is also embarrassed and a little chagrined. Thus one sees again what one had suspected in the first part of the novel; Croft is a gentle, compassionate and reflective man who has no intention of hurting anyone if he can help it.

The View Of Mankind: However, these incidents reveal Croft's personality as being that of a likeable and thoroughly human man, they indicate something less optimistic about the rest of mankind. The old man is quite unaware of the facts of the case, and has simply given himself over to violent emotion. Like Winder, he has an axe of his own to grind; he uses the situation as an excuse to berate the younger generation for not living up to his expectations. One would have every right to expect that an old man like this might have grown gentler and wiser with experience; just the opposite is true, however; he is calling for blood as loudly as anyone. Even the babies are not exempt. Young Tommy hasn't the vaguest idea of what's going on. He is simply fascinated by the things he sees. In this fascination, however, the reader sees what he sees in the adults; a preoccupation with violence and with the weapons of violence. The men themselves, in many cases, have about as much awareness of the situation as Tommy has; they are playing at gunfights, they are easily swayed and are finally carried into the act of riding after the rustlers only by the momentum of the mob and the rhetoric of Tetley. But because they are old enough to ride the horses and fire the guns, disaster will probably result.

The Development: By the end of the second section of the novel, the action is well under way. The progression has been gradual but steady; at the end of Part Two it has become clear that mere human reason (Osgood or Davies), or human good will (Croft and

Gil), or the established legal processes (Judge Tyler), will be unable to stop this progress toward violence. Croft's comments on the weather have paralleled the reader's observations on the riders; the snowstorm is about to break as is a human storm of violence.

Characters: Part Two has added to and confirmed the opinion of Croft and Gil which was formed in Part One. Croft, as usual, is the character revealed in most depth and detail; since he is the narrator, from whose point of view the story is told, the reader can judge his thoughts as well as his actions. His sensitivity was seen in his reactions to the angry old man and to the baby Tommy; his ability to reflect on the situation and make his own decisions is seen in his reactions to Davies' arguments. Croft is impressed by Davies' obvious sincerity and by his logical thinking, but he refuses to accept everything that he says at face value. Instead, he prefers to reflect on these ideas while he is outside, where he feels at home.

Croft's Social Conscience: That Croft has a social conscience is seen in his reaction to Gabe Hart, Winder's handyman. Hart is of barely marginal intelligence, but he has two fixed ideas to which he adheres: his absolute loyalty to Winder, and his absolute hatred of "niggers." Croft would hardly qualify as a member of a modern civil rights group, but he is perceptive in his analysis of Hart's hatred. Croft himself has mixed emotions about Negroes; insofar as he is a man of his time and place, he rather dislikes them, but he also realizes vaguely that this is wrong. He is undecided, then, as to what his reactions to Negroes should be. Eventually in the novel the reader will discover that Croft reacts to the Negro Sparks just as he would to any other fellow human being.

The Other Characters: Davies And Osgood: In Part Two the reader sees Davies and Osgood as similar in their respect for the slow processes of traditional law, and in their relative intellectuality. Even on their first appearance, however, they show obvious and important differences. Croft has respect for Davies. Osgood, on the other hand, is the picture of the ineffectual man of good will. Unlike Davies, he is not strong enough to win the respect of his fellow men in this hard frontier existence. He simply mouths platitudes, and ends by turning the men away from his cause rather than towards it. Osgood seems to be the superficially pious man with little understanding of why he believes what he does; Davies, on the other hand, is the rational man who has worked out every step of his arguments and who is convinced (and is convincing) about their validity and value. He is the ethical rather than the pious man.

Bartlett, Winder And Farnley: These three characters are at once rather complex individuals and the kind of characters one would expect to find in the traditional Western movie or story. None of them is a thinker; they are all violent men and men with private grudges which they are eager to air before the community. Farnley is simply a sorehead - he is convinced that everyone is out to do him harm, and he is eager to do harm to someone else first. Bartlett sounds like the typical small-town demagogue, eager to stir up trouble for its own sake, in an attempt to change the status quo and to control people. Winder is the man who sees progress, in the form of the railroads, as ruining his chance for making a living. He is embittered by this, and anxious to take his vengeance wherever he can.

Moore And Canby: If Osgood and Davies are the peacemakers, and Bartlett, Winder and Farnley the principal troublemakers, Moore and Canby represent the middle ground. Moore is a tough man in his own right, but he doesn't erupt with emotion at any provocation. Canby remains quite aloof from the action; his few ironic comments indicate that he sees the whole situation as so much foolishness. Because he owns the saloon Canby stands on middle ground; he understands the problems of the cattlemen, but he is also able to judge them with some objectivity. He is also, as saloonkeeper, familiar with fights and violence; it is quite apparent that he has little faith in their effectiveness.

Ma Grier And Tetley: Two of the strongest characters in the second section are Ma Grier and Tetley. Though they are barely introduced at this point, the reader knows from Croft's comments on their standing in the community that they are capable of influencing the action of the assembled group. Croft himself is rather doubtful of Ma Grier's motivations; from the description of her the reader begins to suspect that she, like Bartlett and Winder, is perhaps fond of violence because it obscures her own problems - her guilt about a rather sordid past. Ma Grier is not as unreasonable as Bartlett or Winder, however; her fondness for Davies indicates that she is willing to listen to a reasonable argument if it presents itself strongly enough. At the end of Part Two, then, Ma Grier stands as a powerful force which could direct itself toward either peace or complete violence.

Tetley: The same cannot be said of Tetley, however. His calm strength, his grimly cool and ironic demeanor mark him as a man convinced of the correctness of his actions, whatever they might be. Through Croft the reader discovers that Tetley is one of the strongest and most respected men in the community. Tetley's character, too, is somewhat mysterious in Part Two; Croft mentions both his strength and his great coldness. The brief references to Tetley's family, his dead wife and his son, indicate that there is a capacity for cruelty in the man. Tetley, then, stands as a powerful force directed towards violence; the reader suspects that Tetley is seeking this violence for his own motives. Unlike Bartlett and Winder, however, Tetley has not yet made these motives visible. Apparently Tetley is simply the disinterested man acting in the best interest of his community; actually, the reader suspects that Tetley too has his own self-interest uppermost in his mind.

Young Tetley: Tetley's son is an enigma at this point in the novel. We only know that he is bookish and sensitive. It is made clear, however, that young Tetley will figure significantly later in the novel. It is also made quite clear that the motives of the older man center somehow on making his son join the amateur posse. There is some kind of mystery here, then, which the reader rightly suspects will be unraveled in the course of the action in the rest of the novel.

Here the novel begins to take the form of a kind of psychological mystery story as well as of a study in violence and motivations.

The Paralysis Of Gil And Croft: Throughout Part Two the reader has been fully aware that one very strong man, with the right convictions, could possibly have stopped the group from becoming a mob if he had spoken up at the right time. The likeliest candidates for this action are Gil and Croft; they are strong young men who don't mind an argument; they are not too rationalistic, like Davies, too aloof, like Canby, too pious, like the Reverend Osgood, nor too pompous, like Judge Tyler. The indications are strong that, were their own situation different, they might have made a strong attempt to stop the action. But if they are not paralyzed by their own prejudices, like the rest of the characters, they are effectively stopped by the coincidence of their problem: if either of them speaks up too loudly against the lynching, the suspicions of the crowd would probably turn against them, the comparative strangers. And so they are unable to act effectively; they even make an occasional grandstand play to win the crowd over to their side and to quiet any suspicions which might arise. They are obviously innocent, but they are the victims of, and paralyzed by, the circumstances in which they find themselves. Again, the point which Clark is making is quite clear: men of good will find themselves unable to act when confronted by a crisis. Some of the men are paralyzed by their own natures, others by their circumstances. Whatever the reasons for their inability to act, however, the result is the same - the men of violence carry the action.

THE OX-BOW INCIDENT

The action is again low-keyed in the beginning of the third part of the novel. Like Part One, this third section begins with a tranquil description of the beautiful country the men are riding through. Now, however, this takes on ironic overtones, since the riders are engaged in such a completely unbeautiful errand. Croft is again listening to the meadowlarks, picturing in his mind the way the birds fluttered through the grass as he rode the range the previous spring. The contrast between his recollection of the birds, and the present activity, is, though unstated, obvious and striking.

Comment: Conversations: Aside from the beautiful, tranquil description of nature, most of the beginning of this section is taken up with Croft's description of the twenty-eight riders. He gives a fairly detailed description of the actions of some of the men. Croft does not comment on their behavior, but the point is clear to the reader: these men, riding through the beautiful countryside on their errand of death, are

quite oblivious to the significance of their actions. The narrator does not judge them unfavorably - he is, after all, a part of the group - but the reader does.

Young Tetley: Croft relates many of the conversations which he overhears on his ride, but by far the most significant is that which he holds with young Tetley. Tetley's growing bitterness and despair makes explicit what the reader, too, is thinking about the situation; what is even more disturbing is that there is left little room for the possibility of good human action. Croft's reaction to Tetley, like most of his behavior in the book, points to his sensitivity.

Significance: With the conversation between Croft and young Tetley and then Croft and Gil, one sees two possible reactions to posses and lynchings. Young Tetley is the sensitive man, the thinker, who objects to all mob action purely on principle. The young man is thoroughly disillusioned; he has been made submissive to his father's stronger will, but as a result he hates himself, his father, and the whole human race. His view, then, is that of the completely pessimistic intellectual man; men are wolves, ravening after the flesh of other men, and there's not much point trying to resist. Even if one withstood mob justice at one point, another mob would simply be ruling somewhere else. The only answer to a problem like this is destruction, and, in his threat of suicide, young Tetley has made it clear that he chooses to destroy himself. This adds another element of suspense to the novel; the reader, like Croft, is anxious to see whether or not the young man will be able to pull himself out of his depression.

Gil's Response: Gil by this time is just as sick of posses and lynch mobs as young Tetley is, but he is an entirely different kind of man, and reacts in an entirely different way. He is thoroughly practical; the entire endeavor is silly, impractical, ineffective, and is going to mean only that the men will have a hard, long, uncomfortable and unproductive ride ahead of them, for little real purpose. Gil has not the slightest faith that justice, or anything remotely like justice, is going to be done. He, too, however, seems to feel that there is little point in openly rebelling against the posse; among other things, he realizes that the older Tetley is set on carrying out what has been started, for reasons of his own.

Paralysis: Thus, in the reactions of Gil and Tetley's son, one sees two reasons why the lynching isn't going to be stopped. The idealist, young Tetley, hasn't the will power to stop men from actions that he knows are wrong - he can destroy himself, but he cannot take positive action. The practical man, Gil, is simply too practical; he evaluates the situation and decides that it would not be worth the necessary effort to try to stop the men.

Farnley's Vengeance: As Gil and Croft discuss their reluctance to continue the present expedition, another matter becomes clear: Farnley is a man who gives himself over to uncontrolled rages, and has a single-minded desire for vengeance whenever he has been crossed. The gloom of this discussion parallels the gloom of the mountain night; the weather gets colder; the mountain track gets steeper, and the storm's strength increases as the two men consider the doubtful leadership under which they are riding.

Croft And Sparks: Croft's behavior with Sparks is again revealing of his personality. He is a little uneasy, for he has mixed emotions about Negroes; he is ashamed of himself for this, however, and his friendly overtures are an attempt to make up for the way he feels.

This scene adds more depth to Croft's character. Again he is seen as a very human, very sensitive man. He has great sympathy for his fellow men, and he is aware of his own shortcomings. His embarrassment when Sparks refuses his whiskey is amusing, but his insistence that Sparks take the jacket is impressive. It becomes clear that he, unlike some of his fellow riders, is considerate and kind. This emphasizes the irony of Croft's situation - he is the last man in the world who should be found riding out in a lynch mob.

The Stagecoach: The encounter with the stagecoach would be notable if only for its hilarity; it is not only funny, however, but revealing of the men it involves. It is ironic that the posse has been mistaken for bandits because, of course, they have indeed been acting like them - but they hate to have this become so clear. Another comic touch in this scene is the semi-drunken behavior of the stagecoach driver and the guard.

The Wound Itself: the full significance of the wound that Croft received during the mix-up with the stagemen is not really seen until the end of the book, but it can be deduced, at least in part, here. For one thing, it emphasizes Croft's role as observer rather than participant in the activities in the remainder of the novel. Because his shoulder is hurt, Croft can't involve himself in the events that follow, and this makes him more than ever able to comment objectively on what is going on. The wound also sets him apart, to an extent, from the other men. Croft, the sensitive man, has suffered too, just as Davies and young Tetley suffer. The fact that the wound was such a completely unpredictable accident emphasizes another element in the book - the power of chance. It is pure chance that determines whether or not Croft will be wounded, just as it was chance that brought Gil and Croft to town on this particular day and chance that accounts for the presence on the stage of Rose Mapen and her husband. Chance, then, plays an important role in the novel; its significance will increase as the plot develops.

The Trail Again: After the violent encounter with the stagecoach, the rest of the third section is uneventful. The men themselves are somewhat unsure of their position. Thus the third section, unlike the first two, ends quietly; the reader, like the men in the posse, is thinking over the recent events.

Plot Development: Both the plot and the characterization have been significantly advanced in the third section. Step by step, the story has progressed from a simple cowboy tale of fights and gambling to a more and more somber investigation of mob psychology. The transformation of a group of cowhands into a lynch mob is indeed distressing; time and again the reader has sensed that the proper action at the proper time could have averted what is going to happen.

By the end of the third section, however, it has become apparent that things are proceeding inevitably toward a lynching. There is still an element of mystery in the story, however. The story, then, rather than lessening in interest, becomes more engrossing as the action progresses.

Characters: The most important character to be developed in the third section is Gerald Tetley. He was an enigma in the previous section; in his conversation with Croft, however, he reveals himself as the sensitive intellectual who is so appalled by what he sees in mankind that he is utterly unable to act. His domination by his father is made quite clear in his nakedly honest remark to Croft. Gerald Tetley is completely pessimistic in his view of man; men in groups are like packs of ravening wolves, and men individually are unable to act effectively. The only motive that he sees is power. Even women are not immune to this hunger; they cannot often achieve great power by themselves, but they achieve it through their domination of the men they marry.

Significance: Gerald Tetley's significance in the book is clear: he represents the intellectual, the man who understands motivations, who knows where right and justice lie, but who is so involved in his own psychological and spiritual problems that he cannot help himself or others. Unlike many men, Gerald Tetley understands why he acts as he does, yet he is no more a power for good than Farnley or

Winder. He is paralyzed by his pessimism and his low estimation of his own ability.

Sparks: The other major character developed in the second section is Sparks, the old Negro. His personality as it is developed here is no surprise; his character was clearly indicated in the preceding section. Sparks is, however, an interesting contrast to Tetley. If Sparks is not well educated, as Gerald Tetley is, nevertheless he is clearly a naturally intelligent man. He is also wise to the ways of the world; he has no illusions about the goodness of mankind, or about the mission that these men are on. Sparks does not despair, however, as Gerald Tetley does. He simply keeps to his own quiet path, accepting both the good and the evil that he sees around him.

His Position: Sparks occupies a middle position in this strange group. He sees clearly the motivations of the men, and he sees that many of them are evil; however, this does not lead him to pessimism or despair. He sees that his own presence will not be enough to turn the group from their purpose, yet he continues with them; it is enough, for him, that one good, disinterested man should accompany them.

THE OX-BOW INCIDENT

. . . .

Progress: If Part Two began quietly, the fourth section commences on a positively muffled tone. Most of the real activity has ceased, and what little there is hidden by the thick snow which is falling quietly and steadily.

Comment: Gil and Croft are still together as this section commences. Gil is concerned about his friend. Again, Croft is meditating on the nature of the gang, considering its essentially unfriendly and hostile quality. This is an especially striking thought; besides Gil and Croft, there are no real friends in the entire group. One has seen them squabbling among themselves, and making accusations; only the discovery that the rustlers had apparently been found had quieted the dissension among the hunters.

The Ox-Bow: There an implied comparison between the quiet, idyllic serenity of the mountains,

the "Ox-Bow" where the rustlers are hiding, and the turbulence which reigns among the human hunters. Nature, as usual, seems incredibly more beautiful than man.

Donald Martin: It is the young man who is the spokesman of the group of rustlers which the posse discovers, and he is the most interesting character of the three. From his description one judges him to be an appealing man. Thus Martin makes a good effect on the reader; he is in direct contrast to Mapes and Tetley, who had acted like cats playing with a mouse in their refusal to divulge information.

The Explanation: Through the device of the narrator, Clark presents the three rustlers' explanation objectively to the reader. The discussion goes back and forth between the men, and the reader observes it all, making his judgments just as the listening men are doing. Martin's tale, told through Croft, inspires little sympathy or belief from his hearers; to the reader, however, his calm and logical manner, and the appeal of his youth and desperation, are likely to have more effect. The conversation in this part of section four is as suspenseful as a good courtroom scene. One by one, the men bring up objections to Martin's tale; one by one he answers them, only to see his listeners laugh at what he says.

Reactions: The men react to the questions and answers as one would expect from their past behavior. In a sense, the author develops a psychological tightening of the noose through the gradual changes in the men's attitudes to the rustlers, and their reaction to the elements in the unfolding tale.

The Idea Of Justice: One important matter must be cleared up at this point: as Tetley and the others present their case, there is no suggestion that any of these men desire hanging just to kill someone. The whole problem rests, in their eyes, with the slow and undependable nature of "book law"; trials, juries and judges are undependable, and hanging is swift and irrevocable. The background to the whole problem here is part of the background of the West, where, because of the relatively small number of educated persons, because of the vast distances to be traveled, and for many other reasons, justice had in fact often been miscarried. These men consider themselves like the "Vigilance Committees" of Texas; as far as they are concerned they are perfectly justified in taking the law into their own hands, since the law is so undependable. The reader will do well to remember here the coolness with which these cattlemen received Judge Tyler; obviously, the cattlemen feel themselves at least in part victimized by Tyler and his kind. By hanging these three men, who have apparently convicted themselves with their own words, the cattlemen can revenge themselves on rustlers and judges in one action.

The posse are men of action, not words; hanging, in their eyes, seems like the only logical action. Though the reader is not as convinced of Martin's guilt as Tetley and his friends are, he still sees that there is some justification in their decision.

Gil's Protest: If the hanging is partly justifiable, however, the men's behavior is less easy to understand. It is Gil who points out the inhumanity of the proceedings. Gil's protest is especially interesting since it is based on the same grounds that the posse ostensibly stands on; he is a man of action, and he dislikes watching men quibble over other men's lives. By his accusation he implies that Tetley is just another Judge Tyler.

Martin's Reactions: Clark produces a lull following the "verdict" for another investigation of the character of men. There is little activity going on, but with their actions and words the men continue to reveal their own natures, and their prejudices.

Old Hardwicke: Hardwicke's function here is clear; like the old man who berated Croft in Part Three, he reveals the fact that most men are willing to victimize their neighbor, if this will gain them something. Hardwicke is simply a pathetic old fool, and he has been befriended by Martin; even he, however, makes wild accusations.

The Food: The cooking of the rustlers' food is one of the first instances where a real charge of inhumanity could be leveled. Some of the posse are in favor of cooking the food, others, however, are less enthusiastic. To the objective reader, the idea of eating dead men's food seems inhuman; it remains for Donald Martin, however, to make this charge verbally.

Martin's Speech: Martin's impassioned protest is one of the few places in the novel where the issues are stated explicitly. It is especially interesting that Martin refers to the posse as a "pack"; it immediately recalls Gerald Tetley's reference to men as being like a "pack of wolves." Clark, through Martin, is pointedly making the parallel between men who act hurriedly and in groups, and wild animals. The only difference is that the animals can be excused for their behavior, since they are expected to be savage; men, however, are not.

The Vote: The five men who voted against hanging come as a surprise to Tetley; some of them, indeed, are a surprise to the reader. The votes represent the complex character development and skillful shading of motivation that Clark has used - in contrast to the normal black and white western approach.

The Dawn: All of this voting, discussion and argument has been going on against a backdrop of the coming dawn. The author uses this passage of time to add urgency to the situation, since the men are to be hanged at dawn; it is also another instance of the serene beauty of nature being contrasted to the ugliness of man. Croft is himself aware of this contrast; he mentions the feeling, among all the men, that the time for the hanging couldn't really have arrived.

Plot Significance: In terms of plot, the fourth section contains the crisis of the story. It is here that the peak of action is reached. All that follows section four, then, must be anticlimactic from the standpoint of plot.

The Moral Significance: What has not been taken care of in Part Four, however, is the working-out of the moral and psychological significance of these actions. The reader has been aware throughout the novel that there is more involved than mere physical action; now, rather than feeling the story is over, he waits for the meaning of these events to become clear. It has been obvious from the very start that, if the hanging takes place, there will be interesting and important results. So, from a moral and psychological standpoint, the real interest in the novel is just getting a good start. It is this, among other things, which lifts *The Ox-Bow Incident* above the level of the pulp Western; at no point in the novel does the physical action take precedence over the moral and psychological effects of the action.

The Loose Ends: Perhaps the biggest question which the reader still asks at the end of Part Four is about the innocence or guilt of the three hanged men. It has been quite clear that their guilt is still a doubtful matter to at least some of the posse; the reader expects, therefore, that the matter will be cleared up in the following pages. Still another matter is Gerald Tetley's condition, and his previous threat of suicide. The relationship between him and his father has been worsened rather than improved; the reader, then, also wishes to know what will transpire between these two. And of course there is still the question of Croft and Gil; what effect will the day's activity have on these men, whom the reader has come to know rather well?

The Paradox: Thus it can be seen that Part Four is a rather paradoxical, challenging section in this novel. Apparently the action has been completed, and the reader's curiosity should be satisfied. Just the opposite is true, however, and the reader approaches the end of the novel with heightened interest. After seeing the behavior of the men, hunted and hunter; after hearing Gerald Tetley and Donald Martin charge mankind with savagery and brutality, the reader expects some kind of conclusion to be reached about the nature of man.

THE OX-BOW INCIDENT

PART FIVE

. . . .

The overwhelming surprise of Kinkaid's appearance is heightened, not obscured, by the casually understated way in which it is introduced to the reader. The brutality of Kinkaid's inescapable presence stuns the men, as it stuns the reader - this one fact, that he was not killed, changes the entire picture. It reduces the hours of arguing, of wondering about moral right and the processes of the law, of hatred, of questions, of final conviction - to nothing. Kinkaid is alive, the men who did the hanging are murderers. It all seems very simple.

Comment: Chance: Kinkaid's sudden appearance underscores a theme which has been minor but persistent until now - the theme of chance. It was chance which brought Croft and Gil to Bridger's Wells on this of all days; chance led them to the card game and the bad tempers; chance led Amigo to the spot where he saw the "rustlers"; chance determined that Risley, the sheriff, would be out of town. It was

obviously chance which sent Greene off with the news of Kinkaid's death - Greene is just a boy, too young to pause and consider, too young to discover whether his report is rumor or fact. And certainly it was chance which led Martin to Drew's ranch, and which led Drew to forget all his habits and sell the young man his cattle without a bill of sale. In the world of this novel, then, chance - fate, if you prefer - plays a most important role.

Habit: One of the defenses which man uses in the undependable world of chance is habit - the tendency to keep doing things in an accepted way. Drew reveals this tendency when he speaks of the cattle sale. The twin forces of chance and habit are responsible for many of the events in the novel, for in a world of chance man feels safe only if he responds in a familiar way. If the pattern is broken, (by cattle theft and murder, in this case) then men respond violently, defending themselves against the unknown and the unpredictable. Davies, who tries to reason things out, cannot get the men to follow him because reason is too difficult - blind habit, "kill the wrongdoer," is much easier. In this situation, men like Martin become scapegoats - they must be sacrificed in order that the god of Habit be appeased.

Reactions: Again, the men react characteristically when they see that Kinkaid is still alive. Most of them, Gil included, begin to condemn Tetley, loudly asserting that they were forced into the hanging, that they'd thought Martin innocent all the time. To the reader, who remembers the vote, this is simply another example of man's tendency to defend himself, if necessary at the expense of a fellow man. Courage: The Two Voices: As Davies and Croft discuss the hanging, the reader once again hears the voice of the conscience-ridden man (Davies) and the voice of the ordinary man who simply tries to get along as well as he can (Croft). The question of moral courage and weakness is developed with many nuances during this conversation.

The Pack: The reader recalls Gerald Tetley and Donald Martin, and their description of men as a "pack" which should be examined thoroughly as a principal theme of the book. Now, from three quite different points of view, one has heard the same charge leveled. Man alone can be sane and rational, but he is largely ineffective. Man with his fellows is thoroughly undependable, subject to the whims of a leader and even more subject to his own inherent instinct to brutality. Davies' attempt to charge himself with the whole fault is unconvincing; the reader is quite aware that none of the men present could have stopped the mob. The other men's attempts to blame Tetley, however, are equally unconvincing - it was quite apparent, that many of the men were excited by the prospect of a hanging, and that they had taken a good part of the responsibility on themselves. The blame, then, must rest where Gerald Tetley and Donald Martin put it - on "the pack," on men acting without reason, in a group.

Gerald's Suicide: Paradoxically, Croft has just convinced Davies that he cannot accept the full blame for what has happened when he himself assumes the blame for another event - the suicide. Again, in the conversation of these two individuals, a common predicament of man becomes clear: man will always do violence and injustice in mob action, the well-intentioned individual will always accuse himself of the guilt, but the individual will never be really effective against the pack.

Tone: This statement about the collective guilt of man has been made several different ways, by several different people with different attitudes. Gerald Tetley and Davies spoke with desperation; Martin was denunciatory and accusing; Croft, however, in this final section, is simply calm and thoughtful. The author, then, has shown convincingly, from different points of view, that man is responsible for his fellow man but that he has difficulty living up to this responsibility. The tone in this last section is no longer violent; it is, rather, calm and matter-of-fact.

Croft's Comment: Croft, who as usual has retained complete control of himself in this long discussion on the subject of guilt, has the last word. In his comment one can see a final statement on the condition of man: essentially, man is alone; he must face himself and he must make his own peace with reality. However much someone might want to help another person, eventually he must "let him go" to face himself and the world, alone.

Confrontation: The end of the novel is as quiet as the beginning. It is as if there had been too much violence, even for these violent men. The tone of the conversations has become self-consciously cynical; the men, obviously, are unable or unwilling to face the full import of what they have done. As they did in the first scenes, they band together with conversations and drink to avoid looking at themselves or at their actions. Only Davies has forced himself to look and to examine, and Davies, at the end of the novel, is a completely shattered man, unable even to stand without help.

The Scene: The setting for the last paragraphs of the novel is highly ironic. The countryside is as beautiful as it was before; spring is again in the air, and the two riders are again listening to the meadowlarks. The contrast between the peace and beauty of nature and the violence, cowardice and weakness of men is all the more effective because it is not explicitly stated.

Croft: One last look at the narrator is necessary here. Croft is probably the most important character in the novel, since it is through his eyes that all the action is seen. He is stronger than Davies or Gerald Tetley, yet much gentler than people like Winder, Smith or Farnley. Since he is the most balanced character in the novel, his attitude is important. He has no illusions about what has happened; he knows that three men were quite unjustly killed, and that a woman has lost her husband and children their father because of the lynching. He knows that he is at least partially responsible for their deaths, and for the suicide of Gerald Tetley. He has had more than enough of violence. Obviously, Croft is aware of the inhumanity that he has been a part of, and he is aware that this kind of inhumanity will continue.

Yet Croft does not despair. He simply accepts himself, and his fellows, for what they are - limited beings who will go on doing injustices. There remains one constant value for Croft, however, and that is nature. As long as there are meadowlarks in the grass, the last scene implies, Croft will not despair. Nature is good even if man is not, and nature is always there.

Tone: The tone at the end of the novel is one of weariness and acceptance. The story does not end in the violent despair of a Tetley or a Davies, rather it ends in the resignation of Croft, who does not shrink from life even though it is sometimes brutal. The novel cannot be called entirely pessimistic, then, even though its story is tragic. Clark holds out some hope for man; if he will accept himself as limited, if he can look to nature for guidance, then life can continue to have some meaning.

THE OX-BOW INCIDENT

CRITICAL COMMENTARY

Clark's Standing: Although Clark's publications have been rather limited in number - three novels and several short stories - there is no doubting his position as a significant modern American writer. It is never easy to evaluate the position of a contemporary figure, but even a brief glance at the reviews of Clark's books will reveal phrases like "significant contribution to modern literature" and "the best Western novel America has produced."

Source Of His Reputation: His position is due in no small part to the instant success, both critical and public, of *The Ox-Bow Incident*. Clark's reviewers credited him with an agreeably "masculine" style in this book, and with "the ability to tell a story and still suggest meanings beyond the literal." The book was reviewed in all major magazines in America, and almost to a man the critics found it impressive. The reception was especially surprising since this was his first novel; with his disciplined style, spare plot, and clarity of message, Clark betrayed few of the weaknesses often seen in early writings.

Subsequent Appraisals: *The City of Trembling Leaves*, Clark's second novel, received much less praise from critics and public. Here Clark was criticized for being too self-conscious, too allegorical, too obviously message-laden. In his third novel, however, he again scored a resounding success. *The Track of the Cat* was praised for doing successfully what Clark had failed to do in *City of Trembling Leaves*; he told a story almost entirely in symbol, but with great restraint, subtlety and control.

The Short Stories: As a whole, Clark's short stories have won almost universal praise. Several of them, especially "Hook" and "The Rise and Passing of Bar," are considered short classics, and the collection *The Watchful Gods and Other Stories* received good critical notices. Clark has printed short stories in nearly all the significant American magazines, from *The Saturday Evening Post* to *Yale Review*; he has won a large and diversified audience. His wide appeal deserves special notice, since he has not been restricted either to a popular life or an academic one; his novels and stories have appealed both to the mass audience and to the critics.

His Talent: A comparison of Clark's works indicates that his most impressive talents lie in style, structure, and character development. His style, which is spare, efficient and effective, is a superb example of colloquial language disciplined into a medium of art. *The Ox-Bow Incident* is a good example of this. The entire story is told in the words of Art Croft, a relatively uneducated cowhand. The **diction** never becomes inappropriate to the speaker, yet with this unpolished, colloquial speech Clark is able to indicate the subtlest nuances of thought and character. Clark's talent with American western speech as a literary vehicle has always been praised, even in works which were otherwise not well received.

Structure: *The Ox-Bow Incident* again serves as a good example of Clark's ability to structure a novel. His choice of "trite" material - the Western melodrama - reveals rather than obscures this talent, for, using a hackneyed plot, he has written a morality play rather than a potboiler. The utter simplicity of the plot forces the reader's attention to focus on the significance of the events, rather than on the events themselves, and on the personality rather than the actions of the characters.

Suspense: Even with the skeletal plot, however, Clark manages to keep the reader's interest and to build, step by step, a story of suspense which never lets up. Even though the general outline of the plot is often predictable, its smaller twists and turns never are. The reader, in fact, is always conscious that one unexpected action could reverse the entire progress of the tale - indeed, he hopes for such an action. The suspense reaches a peak of tension; then it is relaxed - but the biggest surprise is just to come. After the shock of this surprise there is more tension as the reader ponders Gerald Tetley's fate; he is not surprised by the young man's suicide, but he finds the next suicide another surprise. It is only in the last two pages of the novel that this tension is relaxed, and the reader receives no more surprises. Clark's mastery of suspense and of the amassing of surprises is clearly a contributory factor to his popularity.

Foreshadowing: Clark is not just a master of the surprise, however. Indeed, he has also perfected just the opposite technique; he is very skillful at **foreshadowing**, or preparing the reader for the eventual outcome early in the novel. This **foreshadowing** is a subtler technique than the surprise, and it too is most effective. A good example of this is the description of weather which opens the novel. The narrator describes at great length the unstable quality of this early spring day; he mentions the beauty of the day, but he also dwells on the possibility of winter's return. The unsteady weather with a hint of storm - a storm which eventually strikes - parallels the mood of the men, and the storm of violence which they let loose. It prepares the reader for what happens in the story; it also puts him on his guard, makes him judge men's words and actions more acutely than he otherwise might, for he has been made aware of undependability as soon as the book opens.

Character: Clark's development of character also shows great skill. He does not always develop a character fully - sometimes, as with Rose Mapen, a character may remain a suggestion instead of a real person. Even his sketched-in characters are vivid, however, and the more important figures are complex and highly interesting. Art Croft is perhaps the best example of this complexity. His sensitivity, his love of nature, his honesty, his refusal to rationalize his behavior, his courage and occasional lack of courage - these characteristics and many more make him a truly memorable, truly effective character.

A Critical View: Clark has, during his lifetime, secured a position among the prominent American novelists of the Forties and Fifties. In his *Fiction of the Forties*, Chester E. Eisinger links Clark with both the social and the philosophical novelists; he sees Clark as concerned with the major questions confronting men in society. While not wholly sympathetic to Clark's ideas, Eisinger considers him to be one of the most interesting and significant writers of the last two decades. His criticism is of Clark's view of life, not of his technical skill.

Harry R. Warfel, who considers Clark in *American Novelists of Today*, treats him as a social novelist. He emphasizes Clark's concern, in *The Ox-Bow Incident*, with "the difference between democratic and totalitarian concepts of justice." Another critic, Ernest E. Leisy, mentions Clark as a historical novelist of the

American West. Perhaps the most analytical, and one of the most enthusiastic, treatments of Clark is that of F.I. Carpenter in a short article discussing all his works. Carpenter notes certain artistic weaknesses in Clark's novels and stories, but sees his writing, especially *The Ox-Bow Incident*, as constituting one of the few real tragedies, in the Greek sense, to be written in America.

Thus it can be seen that, though Clark is a relatively young novelist, and has not yet said all that he has to say, he already has a secure position in the world of American letters.

THE OX-BOW INCIDENT

Question: How does the voice of the narrator function in *The Ox-Bow Incident*?

Answer: Clark achieves several different effects by using the person of Art Croft to tell his story. For one thing, his narrator is involved in the action, giving the story a feeling of immediacy. He is also fairly well acquainted with the men and the area, and can thus be expected to be an accurate observer. Most importantly, however, the use of a narrator in the story, rather than some other point of view, enables Clark to tell his story, to convey his message, and still remain completely objective. Croft is established early in the novel as a dependable, honest man who sees clearly and reports the truth. Thus Clark can put into Croft's conversation, and in his thoughts, the ideas which he wishes to convey. Croft convinces the readers without ever becoming **didactic**, or obvious.

Question: How does nature function in the novel?

Answer: Nature is of great importance in *The Ox-Bow Incident*; it is, in fact, almost a separate character in its own right. The most obvious role that nature plays is as a contrast to man; nature has moments of great beauty, peace and tranquility, and these moments are contrasted to the violence, brutality and weakness of man. Nature also has her unpleasant side, however, as is evidenced by the storm in the night. This does two things: it deepens Clark's view of nature (he does not oversimplify things; nature is not all-good and all-kind) and it makes an effective, silent statement about the activities of the men - it is almost as if the storm is nature's attempt to hide the lynching from view.

Question: Does Clark use symbol extensively?

Answer: Clark uses a good deal of symbol in this novel, and he uses it very effectively. Nature, most obviously, can be seen as symbolic of the good which man longs for but can rarely attain; the meadowlarks, which Croft so often thinks of in the height of violent action, are an especially good example of this symbolic yearning for good. The pictures in Canby's saloon are also in a sense symbolic, for they capture the mood of the locality. Even Rose Mapen may be considered a partially symbolic figure, for she too represents a world which these men can rarely attain - the world of kindness.

Question: Is Clark a pessimist?

Answer: This question is a complex one, but important for an understanding of Clark's work. Certainly Clark sees a rather forbidding picture of mankind, and presents it in the book. Three men are hanged for no cause at all; two other men commit suicide because of their responsibility for the hangings; and yet, at the end of the novel, Smith and a few others are set to lynch someone else in an effort to prove their "innocence." The comparison of men to packs of wolves, the accusations about inhumanity, the charges of cowardice - obviously, these statements cannot be simply shrugged off, and man in the novel is guilty as charged. The figure of Croft, however, indicates that the book cannot be read as pure pessimism. Croft is able to recognize his own guilt and still keep on functioning, he is able to turn away from violence, is, in other words, fully human. When he turns to nature it is an indication that Clark sees nature as a source of possible good; if there is any hope for mankind, apparently that hope has its source in nature. Man must keep measuring himself against the natural world; he will always be found wanting, perhaps, but this will keep him from becoming a mere animal.

BIBLIOGRAPHY

WORKS BY CLARK

"Anonymous," *Virginia Quarterly Review*, XVII (July, 1941), 349–69.

"The Ascent of Ariel Goodbody," *Yale Review*, XXXI (December, 1942), 337–49.

The City of Trembling Leaves. New York, 1945.

"Hook," *The Atlantic Monthly*, CLXVI (August, 1940), 223–34.

"A Letter to the Living," *The Nation*, CLIV (June 13, 1942), 679–82.

"Nevada's Fateful Desert," *Holiday*, XXII (November, 1957), 76–7. Nonfiction article on life in the desert.

The Ox-Bow Incident. New York, 1940.

"Personal Interview," *The New Yorker*, XVIII (December 12, 1942), 23–6.

"Portable Phonograph," *Yale Review*, XXX (September, 1941), 53–60.

"Prestige," *The Saturday Evening Post*, CCXIII (April 19, 1941), 14–15.

"The Pretender," *The Atlantic Monthly*, CLXIX (April, 1942), 482–91.

"The Rise and Passing of Bar," *Virginia Quarterly Review*, XIX (January, 1943), 80–96.

"Tale of Hook the Hawk," *Life*, XL (March 19, 1956), 155–8. An excerpt from the short story "Hook."

The Track of the Cat. New York, 1949.

"Trial at Arms." *Saturday Evening Post*, CCXIII (January 25, 1941), 14–15.

The Watchful Gods and Other Stories. New York. 1950.

"The Wind and the Snow of Winter," *Yale Review*, XXXIV (December, 1944), 227–40.

CRITICISM

Brossard, C. "Books," *New American Mercury*, LXXII (February, 1951), 230–4. Review of *The Watchful Gods and Other Stories.*

Carpenter, F.I. "The West of Walter Van Tilburg Clark," *English Journal*, XLI (February, 1952), 64–9. Excellent, if brief, critical analysis of all Clark's writings.

Diers, R. "Are Writers Made, Not Born?" *Saturday Review*, XLVIII (August 14, 1965), 52–3. Brief, penetrating critical sketch.

Eisinger, Chester E. *Fiction of the Forties.* Chicago, 1963.

Leisy, Ernest E. *The American Historical Novel.* Norman, Oklahoma, 1950. Considers Clark briefly as historical novelist.

Lyons, H.H. "Books," *Holiday* VI (October, 1949) 17–18. Review of *The Track of the Cat.*

Portz, John. "Idea and Symbol in Walter Van Tilburg Clark," *Accent*, XVII, 11 2–28.

Wagenknecht, Edward. *Cavalcade of the American Novel.* New York, 1960. Contains brief mention of Clark's significance in the total picture of American novels.

Warfel, Harry R. *American Novelists of Today.* New York, 1951. Good biographical sketch and very brief indication of the scope of his work.

EXPLORE THE ENTIRE LIBRARY OF BRIGHT NOTES STUDY GUIDES

From Shakespeare to Sinclair Lewis and from Plato to Pearl S. Buck, The Bright Notes Study Guide library spans hundreds of volumes, providing clear and comprehensive insights into the world's greatest literature. Discover more, faster with the Bright Notes Study Guide to the classics you're reading today.

See the entire library of available
Bright Notes guides at **BrightNotes.com**

Available in print and digital wherever books are sold

INFLUENCE PUBLISHERS